DATE PLANS
for MARRIED
COUPLES

*One Year of Creative Weekly Date Ideas
to Deepen Your Marriage Connection*

MANDY SHROCK

Marriage In Abundance's Date Plans for Married Couples
© 2022 Mandy Shrock.

Library of Congress Control Number: 2022918915
ISBN: 978-1-958477-04-5 (Hardcover)
ISBN: 978-1-958477-02-1 (Paperback)
ISBN: 978-1-958477-03-8 (Digital Online)

Front Cover Image and Interior Design by KUHN Design Group.

First Printing Edition 2022.

Published by In Abundance, LLC

info@marriageinabundance.com

CONTENTS

MAY

JUNE

JULY

AUGUST

SEPTEMBER

OCTOBER

NOVEMBER

DECEMBER

APPENDIX

FOREWORD

This book of date plans is just "one part of a whole" for Marriage In Abundance's approach to a better marriage. Our goal at Marriage In Abundance is to help couples discover just how deep and meaningful their marriage relationship can be. For best results, this book is to be used in conjunction with *Marriage In Abundance's Devotions for Married Couples, Marriage Challenges for Him*, and *Marriage Challenges for Her*. To find access to the full program, visit www.marriageinabundance.com.

OVERVIEW OF MARRIAGE IN ABUNDANCE:

- Date Plans for Married Couples—weekly date plans for fostering creative, engaging, quality time together.

- Couples' Devotions—weekly studies to deepen your spiritual connection with God and each other.

- Marriage Challenges—weekly suggestions for showing love to one another more effectively, plus monthly suggestions for eliminating unhealthy styles of conflict resolution. As our schedules become overloaded, marital connection takes a backseat. The marriage challenges bring intentionality to meeting one another's needs and desires and spicing up the romance.

INTRODUCTION

I f following Marriage In Abundance's approach to a better marriage, each aspect is to be completed once a week—the date, the devotion, and the marriage challenge. The marriage challenges are to be completed separate from the dates and devotions as they are meant to slip romance into our busy, everyday routines. However, there is more flexibility with the dates and devotions. Some people choose to do the couple's devotions while on their date together—connecting once during the week. Others like to break it up and do their devotions one night of the week and go on their date another night of the week—connecting twice during the week. Choose what works best for you.

Consistency: Regular connection with each other requires determination and intentionality. For the best outcome, it is recommended you, as a couple, decide on a specific day and time each week for your date, put it in your calendars, and stick to it. Consistency keeps you on track. Although sticking to the same day each week is the best way to stay consistent, we know sometimes a consistent time is not possible when you have inconsistent schedules. We—Joel and Mandy—work most weekdays, some evenings, weekends, and even some holidays. So, we look ahead at our calendars and choose a day and time that will work for each week. Then we stick the date in our calendars and make it a priority.

Babysitting: Spending time with your spouse, without the interruption of business, kids, and electronics, is vital to a healthy marriage. You will see a difference in your marriage when you put outside demands on hold and create space for uninterrupted connection. So, hiring a babysitter and setting phones aside during this time is highly recommended.

If hiring a babysitter is not in your budget, here are a few suggestions:

- Have your kids' grandma and grandpa watch them. This is beneficial for both the kids and the grandparents. Studies have shown that kids with grandparents actively involved in their lives are more emotionally stable and have fewer negative behaviors than kids without involved grandparents.

- Trade babysitting with close friends. For example, watch their kids on Tuesdays, then have them watch yours on Thursdays.

- Develop a babysitting co-op. Find four families that want to participate. One family watches the kids of all four families one night a month, then rotate. This gives you three weeks a month to date, and one week a month to babysit. (Hint: when watching many kids at once, it is more manageable when there are planned games and activities for the kids.)

If you don't invest in your marriage while the kids are young, when your nest is empty, your marriage will be also.

The Cost of the Dates: The dates in this book are designed "budget sensitive," so three out of four of the monthly dates can be done for free, or under ten dollars. One date each month will cost about fifty dollars. We know money can be tight and finances are the number one cause for arguments within a marriage. So, if you're at a stage in life where you're really penny-pinching, modify the once-a-month date that costs money.

Planning Ahead: Although the weekly dates are numbered for each month, they are not necessarily meant to be completed in that order. Rainy days would require rearranging the outdoor dates to another week. Also, some dates need supplies bought ahead of time, so you might need to bump those dates back until you've had time to buy the supplies. Look ahead through each month and arrange them to where they work best.

Dates With Intention: This isn't simply a book of date plans for the purpose of having fun together—although, you will be sure to do that! While some of the dates are just plain fun because "fun" and marriage should not be separated, some of the dates go deeper with a focus on serving together within the community, deepening the marriage connection, or spicing it up in bed.

The Value of Creativity: You might notice many of the dates revolve around creativity, design, and art—also intentional. Creativity, or imagining something original, forces us to think outside the box. When we form habits of thinking creatively, we are more likely to search for possible solutions to problems. This mindset inadvertently carries over into problem solving within a marriage. In addition, creativity is connected to emotion. So, being creative *together* increases the emotional bond within a relationship.

Sexual Content: Because this book is designed for dating within a marriage, many of the dates in this book are sexual in nature. Connecting sexually within a marriage is very important. Without it, connection is lost, and spouses become more like roommates. Following Marriage In Abundance's approach to a better marriage, both this date book and the marriage challenges, will keep your sex life interesting and active.

If any of the suggested sexual dates trigger you or make you feel uncomfortable, modify them to your comfort level. If you cannot sexually enjoy one another due to past trauma, please seek professional help. Sex within a marriage is that important.

Due to the sexual suggestions here, it is not recommended to hand this book to your teenager who is looking for a creative date idea.

Open-Mindedness: Some of the date plans will cause you to think, *No way, I'm not doing that!*—not because it triggers a negative emotion, but because it's just not "your thing." Maybe it seems silly or challenges you outside your comfort zone. Many of them seemed silly to the "date testers," but once they gave-it-a-go, they had a blast. So, don't simply chuck an idea because it sounds ridiculous. Studies show people who are open to new experiences have greater passion in life. Bring that to your marriage!

Here's to creative dating and deepening your marriage bond! Let's go!

JANUARY

SYMBOLIC BRACELET CREATIONS

Reminisce with your spouse as you create personalized bracelets for each other. Go to the hobby or craft store together and, using January's budgeted date money, buy the needed supplies—hemp or leather cord, beads, embroidery thread, wire, etc. Personalize your spouse's bracelet.

Ideas: a symbol for a significant memory, your nickname for him or her, a loving statement, an inside joke, encouragement for your spouse.

Once completed, you will each have this reminder of what you share together on your wrists, where you will see it often.

FOR CONVERSATION:

- Do you prefer people text you or call you?
- What was the last text you received that was supposed to go to someone else?
- What do you think I do better than you?
- What inside jokes do we share in our marriage?
- What could I do in the next year to give our marriage a deeper connection?
- Write down ten activities you enjoy. Rate them by how much you enjoy them. Rate them by how much time you spend doing them. Do they match?

BOOKSTORE DATE

Go to your favorite bookstore. Each find a few books about your favorite topics. Settle into a couple chairs next to each other while you peruse through your books. On occasion, share with your spouse something interesting, funny, or inspirational from your book.

> Although simple, this is Joel's and Mandy's favorite date!

FOR CONVERSATION:

- What fictional place would you most enjoy visiting if it were to exist?

- What kids' movie most disturbed or scarred you?

- What is your favorite thing about your current job?

- What's the last thing you did for the first time?

- How did your parents handle differences of opinion? Do you find their way of handling disagreements to be a good example for you? How is the way you handle marital disagreements different than your parents' way?

- What worries do you have that you haven't yet told anyone?

- What would the most romantic evening look like to you?

- Do you like communication during sex? If so, what kinds of things do you like said to you?

WAR ROOM

Watch the movie, *War Room (2015)*. After the movie, discuss these questions:

- Liz said to Tony, "In order for this family to work, we need to communicate." How would improved communication benefit your marriage?

- How did things change when Elizabeth and Tony stopped being "lukewarm"?

- The movie suggested having a "prayer strategy," with prayers over every area of your life. What areas of your life would you include in your strategy? What Scriptures could you pray over these areas? Search for Scriptures regarding those areas of life to pray.

- If this movie has inspired you to have your own "war room," where would be a good place for it?

- What Bible verses would you put on your "war room" wall?

- Clara said, "God showed me that it wasn't my job to do the heavy lifting. No. That was something that only he could do. It was my job to seek him, to trust him, and to lean on his Word." In what area have you been "doing the heavy lifting"? How can you let this go and simply trust God?

- According to Clara, we misplace our perception of who is our enemy, "See, you're fighting the wrong enemy. Now, your husband certainly has his issues, but he's not your enemy. When I fought against my husband, I was fighting against my own marriage and my family." In what ways has Satan snuck in and pit you and your spouse against each other? If you were to view Satan as the enemy and your spouse on your team against him, what would change in the way you dealt with each other? How might your prayers change if you recognized who is the real enemy?

- Let this sink in. Clara taught Liz, "Cause it's not your job! Who said it was your responsibility to fix Tony? It's your job to love him, respect him, and to pray for the man. God knows he needs it. And men don't like it when their woman's always trying to fix them… Elizabeth, you got to plead with God so that he can do what only he can do, and then you got to get out of the way and let him do it." No need for verbal discussion on this but give it some thought. How did things change when Elizabeth stopped trying to do what wasn't her job—fixing her husband—and started focusing, instead, on loving, respecting, and praying for her husband? Consider for a moment: How have I been trying to "fix" my spouse? What actions on your part need to be taken, or ceased, to put Clara's wise words into operation in your home?

- In thinking of situations outside your marriage, how might your response to other struggles change if you didn't see any one person as the enemy?

- Are there people in your life you are trying to control? How might your relationship with them improve if you changed your approach—stopped trying to control or change others, but instead, simply loved, respected, and prayed for them?

- How do we, at times, get in God's way of what he's trying to do with someone?

- More wise words from Clara: "Elizabeth, there's not room for you and God on the throne of your heart. It's either him or it's you. You need to step down. Now, if you want victory, you're gonna have to first surrender." How can you overthrow yourself from the throne of your heart and allow God alone to call the shots?

- At the end of the movie, we hear Clara ask God, "Give me another one, Lord. Guide me to who you want me to help." In what area of life have you experienced triumph? Think of someone going through that same struggle and consider what it would take to come alongside them and help them through their struggle.

ALASKA DATE

This date is about Alaska and its culture. If you live in a cold climate and have always wanted to go ice fishing, now is your chance! If you're like the rest of us and would rather eat cold fries, try one or two of these activities:

- Bake a salmon dish for dinner and Baked Alaska for dessert.

- Build a fire outside to sit beside and go through the questions for conversation. Bundle up if needed.

- If there's snow where you are, build an igloo, or fort, big enough for the both of you, then snuggle inside for the questions for conversation.

- Watch one of these classics filmed in Alaska: *White Fang (1991), Big Miracle (2012), The Call of the Wild (2020)*, or another favorite Alaskan film.

FOR CONVERSATION:

- Because Indigenous Americans of the Pacific Northwest and Canada did not have a written language, they used totem poles to preserve stories. Also, they used symbols to illustrate their family lineages, legends, and ancestors' experiences. Below is a list of animals they frequently used in totem poles and the qualities each animal represents. Go through each animal and its quality and describe a time your spouse demonstrated that quality.

  » Beaver: Creative, Artistic, Determined

23

- » Bear: Strength, Humility, Motherhood, Teaching
- » Bumblebee: Honest, Pure Thoughts, Helpful, Will Power
- » Dove: Peace, Love, Gentleness, Kindness
- » Dragonfly: Fluctuation
- » Eagle: Strength, Leadership, Prestige
- » Halibut: Protector, Strength, Stability
- » Hawk: Forethought, Visionary
- » Heron: Patience, Grace, Easygoing
- » Hummingbird: Loving, Beautiful
- » Loon: Generosity
- » Otter: Trusting, Inquisitive, Bright, Loyal
- » Owl: Wisdom
- » Raven: Enlightener
- » Salmon: Dependable Provider
- » Seal: Intelligent, Organized
- » Wolf: Leader, Values Family

- Which animal do you think best represents your spouse?

- Which animal best represents the qualities of your family?

FEBRUARY

JUST TWO PLAYERS

Together, take a trip to the store and buy a new game that can be played by just two players using February's budgeted date money. Take it home, or to a coffee shop, and challenge your mate to a match. Decide ahead of time the winner's prize. (See Appendix A for suggestions on prizes for the winner.)

FOR CONVERSATION:

- Would you rather have ten kids and two nannies, or four kids but no nanny?

- When was the last time you laughed until your sides hurt?

- If you had to read three self-help books, which subjects would you choose?

- Would you rather have a high intellectual intelligence or high emotional/social intelligence?

- What do you like most about your family? About your spouse's family?

- Have you ever seen something supernatural?

- If you could revisit a past moment with your spouse, to which moment would you return?

- Would you rather increase the quantity or quality of sex?

FOREPLAY
SCAVENGER HUNT

Enjoy a scavenger hunt around your home with a little foreplay at each stop. Helpful hint: Be sure your kids are either not in the house or are sound asleep!

- Prepare ahead of time by buying your favorite "food for licking"—chocolate sauce, whipped cream, etc. You will also need candles, a lighter, and massage oil (or coconut oil).

- You will each hide half of the clues. The husband will solve the first half of the clues and the wife will solve the last half. At each stop, complete the foreplay activity on the back of the clue before moving on to solve the next clue.

- Tear out Appendix D and cut up the clues (without reading them if you like surprises). Give the clues labeled 1-7 to the wife to hide and the clues labeled 8-12 to the husband to hide.

- If you are reading an e-book or have borrowed this book from the library, follow the instructions in Appendix E to make your own clues.

- Tear out Appendix B and give it to the wife. These are instructions for her to hide her half of the clues. Tear out Appendix C and give it to the husband so he knows where to hide the other half of the clues. (If you can't tear out pages, take turns looking at the book or e-book, but don't cheat and peek at your spouse's instructions.)

- Give the wife the candles and lighter to hide with her clues. Give the husband the massage oil (or coconut oil) and "food for licking" to hide with his clues.

- Before you begin the scavenger hunt, put on sexy undergarments underneath your clothes.

FOR CONVERSATION:

- If you could change what falls from the sky every time it was to rain, what would it be and why? Note: It can't be anything of significant value.

- If you could know the future, would you want to know?

- On a scale from one to ten, how happy are you with your physical appearance?

- What was the most physically painful thing you've ever experienced?

- When you are worried, what is the best way I can comfort you?

- In what ways do I make your life better?

- What one thing I wear do you find irresistible?

SNUGGLING & STARGAZING

Drive to a remote location for snuggling and stargazing. For the best view of the stars, go to a rural area, away from city lights. Before you head out, prepare your car, van, or SUV with *lots* of blankets, cushions, and pillows. If you can, remove some seats to make more room for a cozy nest that you both can fit into for snuggling.

- First, stargaze and search for these constellations visible in the February sky of the Northern Hemisphere: Auriga, Canis Major, Canis Minor, Orion, and Puppis (See Appendix F for pictures of these constellations.)

- Next, watch on your phone, "Our God is Indescribable" by Louie Giglio.

- Then, watch a movie while curled up together in blankets. You could use your phone or a portable DVD player if you have one. (Tip: A remote location may not have data, so you may need to download the movie on your phone or tablet ahead of time.)

FOR CONVERSATION:

- If you were paid one million dollars, would you go on a mission to outer space with fifty others to find another inhabitable planet for humans to live?

- If another inhabitable planet were to be discovered, would you be willing to take your family there to live?

- Have you ever seen a UFO?

- Do you think there are other intelligent life forms outside of earth?

- What can you not get right no matter how many times you've tried?

- What was the hardest life lesson for you to learn?

- What lesson came with the biggest consequences?

- Write down five character traits you think you and your spouse have in common. See if your lists match.

- What physical touch best says *I love you* to you?

¡SALSA DANCING!

L earn to dance the salsa. Clear a space in your living room or dining room for a dance floor. Search online for a salsa dancing tutorial for beginners and follow along. First, learn the basic step. Then, pause the video and practice it. Once you both can do the basic step without too much concentration, add more steps and turns. After you've mastered a few steps and turns, turn on some salsa music and dance your hearts out.

Salsa dancing wardrobe: Ladies, wear whatever you have in your closet most similar to the typical salsa dancing attire—short skirt and form-fitting top with flowing sleeves. Men, spruce up in a nice, collared shirt and formal slacks or nice jeans.

If you have time before the date, prepare a bit of cultured food. Search online for the recipes of one or more of these Latin American dishes—chapea, mangú, suspiritos (meringue kisses) for dessert, and morir soñando (milk and orange juice) to drink.

FOR CONVERSATION:

- What is your favorite scent?

- What was your favorite book growing up? What did you like about it?

- What is the most ironic thing you've ever witnessed?

- Would you be willing to leave your current city if your spouse landed a job with higher pay? What pay increase would it take—five thousand more a year? Fifty thousand more a year?

- How far would you be willing to move—one hundred miles? To another country?

- What are your small pleasures in life?

- What is your favorite way to be greeted?

MARCH

BLITHE BOWLING

Go bowling with March's budgeted date money. For each round, use a different technique.

ROUND:

1. Use your non-dominant hand.

2. Roll with your eyes closed.

3. Stand with the lane at your side.

4. Stand on only one foot.

5. Spin in three circles prior to rolling.

6. Roll the ball under and between your legs with your back to the alley.

7. Hop up to the lane.

8. Roll in slow motion.

9. Tiptoe up to the lane.

10. Roll the ball under and between your spouse's legs while he or she stands at the start of the alley.

If you have a reputation to uphold, go bowling without the various techniques.

FOR CONVERSATION:

- If you could change your name, what would you want to be called?

- If you had to choose a different country to have been born, which country would you choose?

- What one thing could you not live without?

- What story can you not retell without laughing?

- Which book has had the most impact on your life and decisions?

- What do you want your last words to me to be?

- Use three words to describe your favorite kind of sex.

VIRTUAL VACATION

Go on a virtual vacation from your living room, taking turns choosing the places to visit. Tip: Using a VR headset would give you the optimum experience. However, if you don't own a VR headset, you can still enjoy a virtual vacation without the VR headset.

There are several options for websites:

360 cities

https://www.360cities.net/

YouTube VR

https://www.youtube.com/channel/UCzuqhhs6NWbgTzMuM09WKDQ

If you have a VR headset, follow these steps to connect.

1. Open the YouTube app and start playing any video.

2. Tap the three-dot "More" icon in the upper-right corner of the screen.

3. Tap Cardboard, then insert your phone into your VR headset.

Jaunt VR

https://www.jauntvr.com/watch/

Discovery VR

https://www.discoveryvr.com/

FOR CONVERSATION:

- Name all the places you have been in this country and around the world.

- Which place was your favorite?

- What was the best souvenir you brought home?

- Who was the most interesting person you met while traveling?

- Do you get homesick while traveling?

- How long does it take before you become homesick?

- Together, make a bucket list of all the places you want to visit.

PUZZLES & PONDERING

Piece together a jigsaw puzzle while discussing the questions below. Jigsaw puzzles may or may not be your thing. Regardless, some of the most meaningful conversations happen over a jigsaw puzzle. We tend to speak more freely when we aren't feeling on-the-spot. The lack of eye-contact helps us feel less vulnerable and more open. It also gives us time for silence and thought.

To take the budget-sensitive route, you could borrow a puzzle from a friend or buy one from a second-hand store. If you have it in the budget to spend extra date money this month, you could order a personalized puzzle ahead of time—a puzzle of a specific interest you share, a meaningful picture of the two of you, or a family picture.

DISCUSSION QUESTIONS:

- What was the most important lesson your parents taught you?

- What was something seemingly insignificant your parents taught you, but it stuck with you?

- Do you share more similarities with your father or your mother?

- What body language does your spouse use when he or she is feeling happy? Upset? Frustrated? Confident?

- Do you feel as if your spouse is able to read your body signals? Or is he or she getting the signals wrong?

- If he or she is getting them wrong, how could you change your body language?

- If you could have talent in a specific area, in which area would it be?

- What is your earliest memory?

- What is your favorite memory from our dating years?

- Which of your dreams most stands out to you?

- What has been your favorite date we've been on together?

- Tell me about your childhood best friend.

- What are your three favorite memories with your childhood best friend?

- Is there a topic you wish I would talk about more freely? (Don't pressure your spouse. Simply mention it.)

- What is my sexiest quality?

- In what ways are you glad you are different than most people?

- In what ways do you wish you were more like everyone else?

- If you could have three wishes granted that didn't involve money, what would they be?

- Have you ever stayed depressed for weeks? How did you come out of it?

- If you could, what one thing would you change about your high school years?

- What was the craziest thing you ever did as a teenager?

- In what ways have you stood up for what you believe in?

- In what ways do you wish you better stood up for your beliefs?

- Do you like a lot of foreplay? Or do you prefer to get right down to business?

- What do you think drives me wild during lovemaking?

AMISH DATE

This date is all about the Amish culture. No technology for your date tonight! Light candles and use your fireplace if you have one.

For dinner, make "haystack." Pile up rice, barbeque beef or taco meat, lettuce, tomatoes, onions, sour cream, cheese, and taco chips.

Another favorite food of the Amish is peanut butter fluff spread on toast or rolls. To make this sweet spread, mix one part peanut butter with one part marshmallow cream.

Play a game I learned from the Amish. Although this game works better with a larger group, it has been modified here for just a two-player game. You will need two pieces of paper, one pencil, and one die. The object is to write the numbers 1 to 100 on your piece of paper before your opponent writes the numbers 1 to 100 on their paper. Roll the die to see who can start writing their numbers first. The one who is not writing rolls the die over and over until they get a "1," at which point, they can grab the pencil and start writing their numbers on their paper while the other person rolls for a "1." When the other person gets a "1," they steal the pencil and continue where they left off. Game play continues until one player gets to 100. (To play with larger groups, take turns rolling the die just once. Steal the pencil when you get a "1.")

To finish off the evening, write a love letter, the old-fashioned way, to your spouse for him or her to keep as a pick-me-up on a bad day.

FOR CONVERSATION:

- What is the worst thing you have ever done to gain the approval of others?

- Describe the last time you felt pampered or spoiled.

- What challenges would you face if you had to live the Amish lifestyle?

- Do you feel content with your life the way it is—your job, the place you live, your friendships, your church, your stage in life, your lifestyle?

- Do you feel you make enough money for your needs? For your wants?

- What dream have you put on the back burner?

- When have you felt most spiritually connected to me?

APRIL

CREATING A CARE PACKAGE

Create and send a care package to someone using April's budgeted date money. Go shopping together and then either ship it to them or deliver it together in person.

For Who?

Think of someone who is going through a hard time, like a soldier overseas, a friend or family member going through a crisis, or an elderly shut-in. Another idea is to give it to someone who is always pouring themselves out for other people, such as a pastor or mentor, foster parents, or that person who volunteers much time and energy to others.

What do we put in the care package?

That depends on their needs. For the shut-in—their favorite treat and a crossword puzzle or activity book. For the soldier—their favorite treats they can only get at home, jerky, powdered drink mix, a movie on a flash drive, a board game. For someone who gives a lot—a gift card to go out to dinner, self-care items such as bubble bath or foot cream, a book of inspirational or uplifting quotes. Search online for gift ideas for the person in their specific situation. Remember, even if you don't "hit the nail on the head" with the items in your package, they will be overjoyed just because you thought of them!

FOR CONVERSATION:

- In what situation have you most felt alone?

- If someone were to make you a care package, what would you want them to put in it?

- Tell your spouse about a time, aside from your birthday or a holiday, someone gave you something that meant a lot to you.

- How do you respond when others hurt you? Has this been a productive way of dealing with the pain?

- In what ways could you better deal with the grief?

- What do you envision when you hear "happily ever after"?

BLINDFOLDED DATE

For this date, you will be blindfolded for almost the whole date. Choose a few of these activities to do blindfolded:

Activities while ONE OF YOU is blindfolded:

- Make a snack while your spouse verbally guides you. (Don't use the stove or knives while blindfolded.)

- Taste test game. The spouse not wearing a blindfold places ten different bite-sized food items on a plate and feeds them to the blindfolded spouse who tries to guess what food it is. Take turns and see who can guess the most out of ten correctly. Be nice in choosing the foods! Also, be sure to lick any lingering flavors off your spouse's fingers.

- Gently rub an object on your spouse's naked body while they guess which object. (You can lay out several different objects ahead of time to make it easier.)

Activities while BOTH OF YOU are blindfolded:

- Have a blindfolded drawing competition. The twist? You spouse is your canvas. Decide ahead of time what you will draw—both drawing the same thing. Take turns drawing it on each other and see who draws it most accurately while blindfolded. **Ideas:** a mama and baby elephant, a car, a spider on a web.

- Have a heart-to-heart discussion while blindfolded. Taking away sight lessens feelings of vulnerability. Share about insecurities, what you love about your spouse, what has been on your heart lately, how your faith is doing, in what area of life you need help, healthy boundaries to protect you and your family, or other heartfelt topics.

- Undress each other.

- Drizzle melted chocolate somewhere on your naked body. Your spouse, then, tries to find it using only his or her tongue. You could play the "hot/cold" game to guide your spouse to the spot.

- If you want to finish the date off with prolonged foreplay and lovemaking, keep the blindfolds on. You will be more tuned-in to sensations.

FOR CONVERSATION:

- What movie quote do you say on a regular basis?

- Do you tend to worry more over past mistakes or the unknown future?

- Name one success your spouse has had in the last seven days.

- What would be the most exciting date ever?

- What is your favorite inspirational quote?

- How could I improve the atmosphere in our home? (Only ask this if you are feeling open to receiving this feedback. When answering, simply suggest without a rant.)

- Is emotional connection before lovemaking important to you? How can I better meet that need?

MINI GAMES

Compete in ten mini-games. Decide ahead of time the prize for the winner—see Appendix A for ideas.

Gather these supplies from around your house: blindfold, cotton balls, two plates, two bowls, petroleum jelly (or glue), scissors, a magazine, a potato, rope (or shoelace), a small stuffed animal, ten plastic cups, pencils with erasers on their ends, a bucket (or large bowl), crackers (or cookies), rubber bands, a spoon, and a deck of cards.

Take turns going first as the last player has the advantage of watching and developing technique.

1. Place the cotton balls on one plate. Set the other plate next to it. Put a dab of Vaseline (or glue) on your nose. Move the cotton balls from one plate to the other using just your sticky nose. The player who moves the most cotton balls in one minute wins this round.

2. Choose a page in the magazine that would make a good puzzle (or print a picture you find online). Both players have a chance to look at the picture before it gets cut into pieces. Then, cut it into about twelve pieces. Take turns putting it back together. Time each other—the player who completes the puzzle in the least amount of time wins this round.

3. Push a potato across the room with just your nose. Time each other—the player who gets it to the goal in the least amount of time wins this round.

4. Tie the rope (or shoelace) to your back belt loop. (If you're not wearing pants with a belt loop, put on a belt and tie

it to that.) Tie the small stuffed animal to the other end of the rope at a height so it's dangling a few inches from the floor. Place the cups in a row, about six inches apart. Knock over the cups with the stuffed animal using only the momentum from swinging your hips. Time each other—the player who knocks over all the cups in the least amount of time wins this round.

5. Land a pencil into a bucket (or large bowl) by bouncing it on its eraser end. The player with the most pencils in the bucket after one minute wins this round.

6. Stack crackers (or cookies) one at a time on your forehead while tipping your head up. The one with the most stacked crackers remaining on their forehead after one minute wins this round.

7. Build a pyramid with the cups. Then, standing or kneeling six feet away, knock the cups down by shooting rubber bands. The player who knocks down the most cups within one minute wins this round.

8. Blow a cotton ball across the table into a bucket (or bowl) placed on its side. If the cotton ball falls off the table, it is placed back at the starting line. Time each other—the player who gets the cotton ball in the bucket in the least amount of time wins this round.

9. While blindfolded, transfer cotton balls from one bowl to another using a spoon. The twist? The bowl filled with cotton balls is placed in the player's lap. The player holds the other bowl—the one to be filled—on his or her head. The player with the most cotton balls in the bowl on their head, after one minute, wins this round.

10. Build as many houses of cards with four walls and a roof as you can. The player with the most card houses standing after one minute wins this round.

FOR CONVERSATION:

- What kind of monster were you afraid of as a child?

- What is your favorite movie genre?

- Why do you think you are drawn to this genre?

- Is there a group you wish you were a part of?

- If you were given one thousand dollars to throw a party for all your friends, describe what that party would look like.

- Which past relationship taught you the most?

- What is your biggest insecurity? How can I help you overcome that?

- What do I do that turns you on, but I am unaware of its effect?

HIPSTER DATE

This date is all about the hipster subculture. To quickly summarize, hipsters are usually in their thirties. They tend to be humanitarian pacifists, value learning new things, promote "reduce, reuse, and recycle," take pleasure in the restoration of old things, admire the arts, eat "clean," and enjoy non-mainstream music.

Choose one or two of these activities for your Hipster Date:

- Go shopping at a second-hand store or garage sale for something to repurpose.

- Make a blog or vlog together about a topic you're passionate about, then post it on social media.

- Learn something new from an internet tutorial.

- Visit your local Habitat for Humanity ReStore and buy something "new" for your house.

- Read or write poetry to each other.

- Prepare a vegan meal together.

> Listen to an indie rock mix station during your date.

FOR CONVERSATION:

- Have you ever changed your course of action based on a dream you had?

- What is the strangest thing you have done in another person's house?

- When was the last time you were pleasantly surprised?

- What was the last show you binge-watched or the last book you couldn't put down?

- Show me your favorite meme.

- "Hipsters" want their material goods to add an element of meaning to their life, with stories and values attached. Name a material good of yours that has a story to go along with it.

- Hipsters are about pacifism. How could we be better keeping the peace within our marriage?

MAY

A LIVING TRIBUTE

Plant a tree together as a symbol for your marriage using May's budgeted date money. If it can't be planted in your own yard, try planting it in a place you will see it on occasion and be reminded of your growing marriage—perhaps the yard of a parent, sibling, or close friend. Together, go shopping at a nursery to pick out the perfect tree, then get to planting. As you water the tree over the next few days, think about how you plan to nourish your commitment to one another.

Planting a tree is an ancient tradition practiced by various cultures to celebrate a marriage. The planted tree represents roots established, growth, resilience, and a heavenward pursuit. Just as a tree bends in a storm, so we weather the daily struggles of life, but come out of the storm stronger.

If you have been through a rough patch in your marriage, now would be a good time to renew some vows to each other using the tree to symbolize your renewed promises to each other.

> *"Never cut a tree down in the wintertime. Never make a negative decision in the low time. Never make your most important decisions when you are in your worst moods. Wait. Be patient. The storm will pass. The spring will come."*
>
> ROBERT H. SCHULLER[1]

FOR CONVERSATION:

- What was the best thing that happened to you this week?

---

1. "Robert H. Schuller Quotes." BrainyQuote.com. BrainyMedia Inc, 2021 August 202https://www.brainyquote.com/quotes/robert_h_schuller_393754

- What compliment did you most enjoy receiving this week?

- If you were to write a personal ad about yourself, what would it say?

- If you could go back in time, what would you change about your first year of marriage (your own actions—not what you wish your spouse would change)?

- What area of your marriage needs nurturing?

- If you were to rewrite your vows, what would you write?

BET ON PEOPLE

G o to a place teeming with people, like the mall or another crowded place. Find a place to sit together and do one, or both, of these activities:

PEOPLE WATCHING PRESUMPTIONS:

Decide ahead of time what the "prize" for the winner will be—see Appendix A for ideas. Place bets on people's behavior. Here are some examples, but feel free to make up your own:

- Sit near an escalator and bet on which individuals will stand on the escalator and which will walk up them.

- Sit near a door. Guess what percent of people will open the door for others.

- Bet on the percent of people who will be looking at their cell phones as they walk.

- Guess how many people you will see with a certain hair-style, like a mullet, man-bun, or dreads.

- Bet on how many people you will run into that you know.

- Make up your own as you go.

PEOPLE-WATCHING PERCEPTIONS:

See if your spouse can guess who you're describing, using abstract, opinion-based descriptions. For example:

- "Someone who looks like Tom Cruise."

- "The person wearing the sweater that's my style."

- "The guy who looks like he could take down a professional wrestler."

- "The couple who looks like they're on their first date."

FOR CONVERSATION:

- How many scars can you count on your body? Are there any you haven't told me the story?

- What qualities do you think make a good boss versus a bad boss? Do you think you have the qualities to be the "good boss"?

- Do you have any accomplishments you hope to achieve before you die?

- What song do you think is most relatable to the way you feel about me?

- Gauging from my response, what do you do to me during lovemaking that I like the most? How can you tell?

PICK UP A KNACK

earn a new skill by watching an online tutorial.

Ideas: how to sketch, the latest dance trend, life hacks, how to juggle, photography tips, origami instructions, cooking tips, how to draw caricatures, self-defense, magic tricks, how to speed read, how to improve your memory...

FOR CONVERSATION:

- What is the most unique skill you have learned?

- What is something you have always wanted to learn but didn't have the time or patience for it?

- What have you tried to learn but gave up on? Do you think you'd ever want to try again?

- What small gesture from a stranger renewed your faith in humankind?

- What was the most recent thing you formed an opinion about?

- What about you do you wish I more often showed appreciation?

SLOWIN' DOWN FOR COUNTRY TIME

This date is all about life in the country—slowing down and enjoying nature. Find a peaceful, public place in a rural area: a grassy field, a wooded park, a river, or a creek. If you live in a city, drive out to the country.

Choose a couple of these slow-paced activities:

- Have a picnic.

- Lie on a blanket and listen to nature.

- Skip stones.

- Make a chain of wildflowers into a hair-wreath or necklace.

- Walk through a creek.

- Play your favorite two-person game on a blanket.

- Learn country line dancing by watching an online tutorial.

FOR CONVERSATION:

- If you don't live in a small town, do you think you would enjoy living in one?

- What are, or would be, the pros and cons of living in a small town?

- How often do you need to be alone?

- When alone, how long does it take before you begin feeling lonely?

- If you had an entire day to be alone, what would you do?

- Do I make you feel like you are a priority to me?

- How could I make you a higher priority?

JUNE

CONTRIBUTION TO THE KIDDOS

Contribute to the kids in your life using June's budgeted date money.

If you DON'T have children:

Invite nieces, nephews, or kids of a close friend to the movies. Children's movies are fun—especially when justified by taking a child! (Certainly, their parents would love the date night as well.)

If you DO have children or grandchildren:

Create something for the kids on your date to later surprise them. **Ideas:** a climbing wall fastened to a tree, a tire swing, a gymnastics beam, stilts, a skate ramp, a dollhouse, a zip line, a long slip and slide with plastic sheets, a costume, a tent-like reading nook, a toddler kitchenette from an old entertainment center, a painted chalkboard wall.

FOR CONVERSATION:

- What was your favorite hand-crafted item you had as a child?

- What was your favorite movie as a child?

- What was your favorite game or activity as a child?

- What question would you most like to know the answer, but haven't yet found?

- Do you grow and mature more through hearing praise and affirmation or through listening to another's perspective?

- What part of our marriage would you want our kids to emulate?

STRIP VIDEO GAMES

Hijack your kids' video gaming system for this date. If you don't have a video gaming system in your home, play an online game using your computer or phones. Every time you die or lose a round, strip off an article of clothing.

FOR CONVERSATION:

- What is your favorite outfit of mine?

- When was the last time you were bored?

- What's the first thing you do when you are bored?

- What have you had to learn the hard way multiple times?

- What is your favorite Bible story?

- What in our schedule do you most want to change?

- Describe an evening out with me that would put you in the mood.

OUTDOOR CHALK ART

Create an art mural using sidewalk chalk on your driveway, side-walk, or back patio. Not the typical sunshine, rainbows, and stick figures you see on driveways created by kids, but the in-depth, detailed, and profound art you see at art festivals. For inspiration, search "chalk drawing ideas."

FOR CONVERSATION:

- Which art creation of yours are you most proud?

- Would you rather your spouse write you a poem or draw a picture of you?

- Would you rather receive compliments or a massage?

- Talk about the biggest rejection you've ever felt. How did you rise above?

- If I really need attention from you, what could I say to get that?

- If you could choose an outdoor setting for sex, and privacy was a given, which would you choose: waterfall, jungle, beach, large square raft in the water, forest, flowery meadow, wooly rug by a campfire?

- If you could choose an indoor setting for sex, which of these places most fancies you: hut on a private island, yacht, cabin in the mountains, treehouse, luxury hotel, penthouse suite overlooking a large city, the mile-high club?

THE BIG CITY

This date is all about life in the big city. Drive to the nearest big city and choose a couple activities from this list:

Free or minimal cost:

- Walk downtown, explore, window shop, and watch the street performers.

- Join a walking tour. Most big cities offer free walking tours. (Remember to tip!)

- Bring along your bikes and bike downtown.

- Visit an ethnic market and taste a food you've never tried.

- Take a stroll through a city park and people watch.

If you have extra money in your budget this month:

- Take a city tour by bus or trolley.

- Visit a popular place unique to that city.

- Go to a jazz club.

FOR CONVERSATION:

- If you don't live in a big city, do you think you would you enjoy living in one?

- What are, or would be, the pros and cons of city life?

- Which do you prefer: large gatherings, a double date, or a one-on-one visit?

- Do you have memories of your parents arguing as a child?

- Discuss the type of conflict resolution you saw between your parents.

- What would it look like for you to emulate the beneficial and effective styles of conflict resolution you saw growing up?

- How can you change ineffective conflict resolution within your own marriage?

JULY

WHATEVER FLOATS YOUR BOAT

Visit a nearby state park which rents boats using July's budgeted date money. Depending on your budget, rent paddle boards, kayaks, a canoe, or a paddle boat. Spend the day floating and relaxing together.

FOR CONVERSATION:

- What is your favorite memory involving water?

- Would you rather have a meal at a romantic five-star restaurant in Paris or an outdoor restaurant on the beach in the Bahamas?

- If you could choose to be an expert on a given topic, which topic would you choose?

- How do you usually handle people you don't like?

- Who has been most influential regarding the path you chose in life?

- What is the biggest sacrifice you've made for our marriage?

TRUST ACTIVITIES

Assure your faith in one another through a few of these trust-building activities:

- **Vision Board.** Go through magazines and cut out images and phrases that express what you want for your future together. Use them to craft a vision board.

- **Eye-Gazing.** Find a comfortable position where you can look into each other's eyes for at least ten minutes without saying anything. Though this exercise *seems* silly (and causes awkward laughter the first few minutes), once you push past the absurdity, it connects, builds trust, and releases pent-up emotion. Let the emotions surface. Afterward, discuss what you felt: vulnerability, passion, peace, curiosity, etc.

- **Blindfolded Obstacle Course.** Create an obstacle course. Then guide your blindfolded partner through it, either verbally or by holding hands. **Ideas:** rearrange the furniture, use pillows they must step over, place cups randomly they should not kick over.

- **Important Tips:** If you rearrange the furniture, let them know so they expect the change. Block off any areas that could be harmful, like the stairs, trip hazards, or sharp corners.

- **Guided Tasks.** Guide your blindfolded spouse through a task, using only gentle words. No yelling or expressions of frustration. **Task ideas:** tie a tie, put together a pre-school puzzle, or complete a simple craft.

- **Guided Sketches.** Sit back-to-back. One spouse holds a simple cartoon-type image while the other holds a paper and pencil. The spouse holding the picture gives verbal instructions for the sketcher who recreates the picture.

- **Empathy Exercise.** Tell your spouse about a difficult event from your life. Simply state the facts, leaving out your feelings. Have your spouse retell the event, adding in how he or she thinks you must have felt during each part of the story.

- **Synergetic Walk.** Walk from one side of the room to the other, side-by-side. For the first round, stand a couple feet apart and lean into each other, shoulder-to-shoulder. For the second round, walk side-by-side holding a balloon or small pillow between your ankles. For the third round, walk holding the balloon or pillow between your hips.

FOR CONVERSATION:

- What was your worst nightmare?

- What are your top two favorite subjects to talk about?

- Is there anything for which you have trouble forgiving yourself?

- What do you need to do to forgive yourself and let it go?

- If you could have God answer one question, what would it be?

- What are my five greatest strengths?

- In what ways could I be using those strengths that I'm not already?

LIBRARY DATE

What topic have you been wanting to learn more about? Go to the library and each find a book on that topic to read later or an audiobook to listen to on your work commute or while running errands. While you're at the library, grab a movie to watch together when you get home.

To spark ideas: your hobby, parenting techniques, home repairs, soap making, developing personal boundaries, organization and minimalization, an interesting historical event, holiday tradition ideas, tips for success in life, how to be a better friend, money management

FOR CONVERSATION:

- If you could bring a mythical creature to reality to be your pet, which creature would you choose?

- What's the craziest thing you've ever done? Would you do it again?

- Talk about an emergency situation you were a part of. How do you think you handled it?

- Movies have a conflict followed by a resolution. What conflict and resolution in your life could make a blockbuster movie?

- In what way could I honor you above myself?

- What is your favorite sexual memory with me?

CHILLIN' & GRILLIN'

Cook your dinner outside—on a grill or over a bonfire—at a park or in your backyard.

Ideas for Grilling: traditional grilling foods, like burgers, brats, hot dogs, and corn on the cob, OR something different for the grill, like steak, salmon, mini pizzas, shrimp, asparagus, zucchini, eggplant, portabella mushrooms, plums, or even peaches!

FOR CONVERSATION:

- If you were given fifty-thousand dollars, what would you buy?

- What do you regret not doing as a child?

- If you could choose to have your own personal "Jiminy Cricket"—sitting on your shoulder, helping you choose right from wrong, and offering wisdom—would you choose that? Why or why not?

- At a large social gathering, do you prefer the spotlight or one-on-one conversation?

- If you had to teach a class, what topic would you teach?

- What is your greatest need right now?

- How could we meet both our needs?

AUGUST

DRIVE-IN MOVIES WITH PRE-SHOW BINGO

Go to a nearby drive-in movie using August's budgeted date money. Get there early. While you wait for the movie to start, have a mini scavenger hunt to see who can spot these first:

- a person with red hair
- an out-of-state license plate
- a couple displaying physical affection
- an animal
- a person wearing a hat
- a sports logo
- a black truck
- a license plate containing the letter, "J"
- a person eating popcorn
- a vehicle holding five or more people inside
- a convertible
- a person sleeping
- the American flag
- a person you or your spouse knows
- a person running

FOR CONVERSATION:

- Did you go to the drive-in movies as a kid? What movies do you remember seeing?

- If you only had one day left to live on earth, what would you do?

- What was the most recent awkward moment you experienced that I don't know about?

- When was the last time you sang when you were alone? When was the last time you sang with others?

- Have you ever read a book that changed your life? What book and how did it change you?

- What could I do to better communicate my thoughts and feelings to you?

BOUDOIR PHOTO SHOOT

Spice it up with a boudoir photo shoot of her, taken by him. Since men are visual beings, this date satisfies his desire for visual excitement—with the one to whom he should be going for that desire—his wife alone. Ladies, before you chuck this date, please read it fully. There are options. Nudity is not the only option for this date to be a winner for you both!

Instructions found in Appendix G.

FOR CONVERSATION:

- What was the most expensive thing you ever bought?

- How did your childhood friendships change as you grew older?

- If you were given a Saturday free of all responsibilities, and your family was busy, would you rather spend it alone or with one best friend?

- What five traits do you believe are most important for everyone to have?

- Do you prefer to be the pursuer or to be pursued?

- Name a place you'd love to have sex that we haven't yet.

- What makes you feel secure and provided for?

ART DISTRICT EXCURSION

Take a stroll through your local art district. If you're unsure where it is, search for it online. If your local art district has a calendar of events, search for an event that interests you and plan your date for that day.

FOR CONVERSATION:

- What is your dream car?

- Think about the last time you were so excited, your heart felt like it was going to beat out of your chest. What caused that excitement?

- Who was your first crush? What did you like about him or her?

- What was the craziest or most interesting conversation you overheard?

- What qualities do you most value in a best friend?

- Whose marriage do you most admire? Why?

LONG LIVE GAME NIGHT

Hang up your hat at home and settle in for a long-lasting game. Play Monopoly, Risk, Civilization, or another game that takes a while and will last through your date. See Appendix A for ideas for a winner's prize.

FOR CONVERSATION:

- What game most angers you when you lose?

- If you could choose only one store, other than a grocery store, to shop for the rest of your life, which store would you choose?

- If you were given fifty-thousand dollars and had to use it to start a new business, what business would you start?

- For New Year's Eve, would you prefer a big party or just the two of us at home?

- Name something you've always been able to count on me for.

- Would you rather, within one week's time, have three quickies or just one night of romance and lingering lovemaking?

SEPTEMBER

PROGRESSIVE REMINISCENT PICNIC

Trigger the memories of your relationship by revisiting the special moments that started it all—the places where you first met, went on your first date, shared your first kiss, and became engaged. If you're not within driving distance to those places, recreate a similar setting as best as you can. For example, if your first kiss was by a fountain in the park, visit a park in your city with a fountain.

If one or two "first places" involved a restaurant, use September's budgeted date money to eat in those restaurants. If your "firsts" did not involve a restaurant, pack a picnic to eat progressively with an appetizer at the place you first met, main course at the place of your first date, and dessert at the place of your first kiss or place of engagement.

The discussion questions are divided into segments so you will reminisce each event at each stop.

DISCUSSION QUESTIONS:

At the place you first met:

- What was your very first impression of me?

- How am I the same as that impression? How am I different from that first impression?

- Do you remember who I was with, what I was wearing, or my hair?

At the place of your first date:

- What thoughts were running through your head on our first date?

- What made you want to go on a second date with me?

- Which date was your favorite from our early dating years?

- At what point did you know you were in love with me?

At the place of your first kiss:

- Before our first kiss, did you expect we would kiss on that date? Or were you surprised?

- What thoughts were running through your head right before we kissed? What were your thoughts during the kiss?

- What feelings did you experience when we first kissed?

- Re-enact your first kiss.

At the place of your marriage proposal:

- At what point did you know you wanted to marry me? What caused you to be certain?

- Do you remember how the question was asked? Do you remember the exact words of the response?

- What feelings were you experiencing during the proposal?

- Reminisce your announcement to your family and friends. How did they respond?

- How do you think you have changed for the better since we got married? How have I changed for the better since we married?

GEOCACHING

Geocaching is an outdoor treasure hunting game using GPS (your cell phone will work). Navigate to a specific set of GPS coordinates and then search for the geocache, which is a hidden container at that location. You can do this for free at www.geocaching.com or by downloading the geocaching app. If you find that you love it, you can upgrade your membership for a small fee that will give you additional features and more caches to hunt. At its simplest level, geocaching requires these steps:

1. Register for a free Basic Membership.

2. Search for caches nearby or in an area you would enjoy hiking.

3. Click on the name of the cache you would like to check out.

4. Get the coordinates.

5. Enter the coordinates in a mapping app on your phone or use the geocaching app to find the location.

6. When you find the cache, sign the logbook that's inside, then return the geocache to its original location.

7. Optionally, you can share your geocaching stories and photos online.

Tips:

- When choosing a cache to hunt, pay attention to the distance you will hike, the terrain difficulty, and the how hard it is hidden (labeled "difficulty"). Choose a cache based on the levels you are comfortable with.

- Once you find the coordinates, the caches are not in an obvious location (think in a hole in a tree, under a bench, in a birdhouse, under a pile of rocks).

- You may need a bug deterrent.

- Watch for poison ivy.

FOR CONVERSATION:

- What is your biggest pet peeve?

- Before marriage, were most of your friends girls or guys?

- Besides money, what tangible item would you be willing to go on a week-long "treasure" hunt for?

- Which character in a tv show or movie do you think resembles your own personality? Which character resembles my personality?

- With which acquaintance do you wish you were closer friends? What could you do to foster that friendship?

- What conflict have we had in our marriage that turned out productive and favorable for us both?

YOU'VE GOT... PERSONALITY!

Take a few different personality tests online, then go over their results together. The results will give you a better understanding of both you and your spouse—what causes his or her thoughts, motives, and actions. Understanding these aspects of your spouse helps you better communicate and connect. There are many tests to choose from and most of them can be found online for free. Here are a few well-known personality tests, but feel free to use another: The Myers-Briggs Type Indicator, DiSC, The 5 Love Languages, Spiritual Gifts, Berkeley Emotional Intelligence, Empathy Quotient, The Big Five Personality Traits, Career Personality Profiler, Cattell's 16 Personality Factors.

FOR CONVERSATION:

- Which result of your personality test surprised you?

- Does your current job match your personality results?

- If you had to choose three things you own to represent your personality, what would they be?

- What personality differences do we have? How can we make them work well together?

- How do you typically show affection? Is it different than the way you receive affection?

- Under what circumstances do you turn to me for help? How do I typically help? How could I better help?

AFFIRMATIVE LETTERS

G o to a coffee shop and write letters. Each write separate letters and then share them with one another at the end.

If you have children or grandchildren:

Write each of them a letter with only positivity. If they're too young to read, write a letter and set it aside for them to open in the future, when they are teenagers or are graduating. Include how you felt the day they were born, what you want them to know about you, what you desire for them to have in life, who is the most influential person in your life and why, what traits in yourself, or their other parent, you want to see carried on in them, how proud you are of them, what good qualities you see in them, and what you hope for their future, etc.

If you don't have children or grandchildren:

Write a letter of encouragement to someone close to you—a niece or nephew, a sibling, a close friend, a parent, or a mentor.

FOR CONVERSATION:

- Share your letters with each other when you're done writing.

OCTOBER

A-MAZE-IN CORN

Visit a nearby corn maze using October's budgeted date money and get lost together. If you're not located in the half of the country that grows corn, find a fall festival to enjoy together.

FOR CONVERSATION:

- If you had to choose one of these people as your life coach, who would you choose: Oprah, Walt Disney, Mark Zuckerberg, Steve Jobs, Mother Teresa, or Arnold Schwarzenegger?

- Summarize your favorite fictional book to your spouse. Then put your heads together to come up with a different ending.

- What is the most ridiculous thing you were tricked into believing?

- What do you think people *should* be more worried about?

- What do people tend to worry about that they shouldn't?

- What do you think I could be doing differently to better enjoy my career?

YOUR CANVAS LOVER

Use body paint to turn your spouse into your art project. Let your mind run free as you paint his or her body as a canvas of art.

Ideas: paint a vine of flowers over limbs, a beautiful landscape or animal over the "canvas" of the back, sexy garments, his or her favorite sports team logo, or something pertaining to his or her interest or hobby.

To add spirituality, paint a Bible verse covering your spouse. Pray it over him or her as you paint it. Use your favorite verse or one of these suggestions: Jeremiah 29:11, Deuteronomy 31:6, John 16:33, Philippians 4:13, Isaiah 41:10, Romans 8:37-38, Romans 15:13, Philippians 4:7, Psalm 29:11, Matthew 11:28, Psalm 94:19.

FOR CONVERSATION:

- Who in your life do you consider having the most success? What makes him or her successful in your eyes?

- What is the strangest date you've ever been on?

- What about yourself would you like to see from an outside perspective?

- Name a personal rule you have given yourself.

- What was the most dangerous thing you have done?

- In an ideal world, how long would foreplay be?

PASTOR APPRECIATION

October is pastor appreciation month. A pastor's energy is more often *drained* than *filled* by others, and pastors typically receive more *negative* feedback than *positive* feedback. Pastors need encouragement!

Here are some inexpensive ideas:

- Make them a meal they can heat up on a busy day.

- Bake them a pie.

- Tell them you and your spouse are doing a "service" date and ask how you can serve them. For example, rake their leaves, power-wash their deck, paint a room in their home, or do another house project for them.

- Remodel their office(s), with permission.

- Decorate their office(s) with balloons, a "thank you" banner, streamers, and their favorite treats.

- Invite them over for dinner.

If you have extra money in your budget:

- Go shopping and assemble a care package for them.

- Take them out to eat for your date.

Whatever you choose, include a thank you card to express your appreciation. If pastors aren't told they are appreciated, they will never know! This is probably why Paul wrote, "Now we ask you, brothers and sisters, to acknowledge those who work hard among you, who care for you in the Lord and who admonish you. Hold them in the highest regard in love because of their work. Live in peace with each other" (1 Thessalonians 5:12-13).

FOR CONVERSATION:

- Would you rather have the ability gain all the knowledge contained in a book by simply picking it up or be able to eat as much as you want without ever gaining weight?

- To which Bible story do you most relate?

- What was the most frustrating experience you have had?

- What topic could you talk about for hours?

- What is the most surprising self-realization you've had?

- What part of church do you like the most—music, communion, the sermon, connecting with other believers, serving, something else?

- Which pastor has been the most influential in your life & why?

SECOND-HAND STORE SCAVENGER HUNT

Go to your favorite second-hand store and compete with your spouse to find the listed items in Appendix I. Decide ahead of time the winner's prize—see Appendix A for ideas. Tear out the pages of Appendix I and give one to each spouse. If you cannot tear out the pages, duplicate them. If you're using an e-book, take a screenshot and send it to your spouse.

When you get to the store, set a timer on your phones for forty-five minutes. Go your separate ways to search for the listed items. When you find them, take a picture of them using your phone. When your forty-five-minute timer goes off, meet at the front door, then go out for coffee or dessert while you go through your pictures and tally up your scores. One more rule: When you find an item, put it back how you found it. Don't hide it or move it to another location.

FOR CONVERSATION:

- What is more important to you—fashion or comfort?

- What was the dumbest thing you ever did?

- Would you rather be a doctor with average income or work in a factory with double the average income?

- On which subject could you spontaneously give a half hour presentation with no prep?

- Name two things you like about yourself.

- Name two things you want to change about yourself.

- Have there been times when you initiated, and I didn't get the hint?

NOVEMBER

BUY-A-DATE

Go buy your date using November's budgeted date money. Typically, the date plans we give you include a list of ideas, but the concept of this date isn't to go to the store with a particular item in mind. Half this date is combining *your* creativity at the store. The other half is enjoying your purchase.

FOR CONVERSATION:

- What do you wish you had more time for?

- How do you get in the way of your own success?

- Who in your life has had the worst series of unfortunate events?

- What is the most absurd conspiracy theory you have heard?

- Are you aware of any problems in your life that need attention but feel you are not prepared to deal with them? What do you think you need to deal with them? How can you get to that point?

- If money were not an issue, what gift would you buy me?

FREEZER MEAL PREP

Assemble freezer meals together to prepare for the upcoming busy season. You'll thank yourselves later! Toss some ingredients into gallon zipper bags, then freeze them. On a day you know you won't have time to cook, stick your freezer meal in the crock pot that morning. Recipes can be found in Appendix J—but feel free to search for other freezer meals online.

If you have a total of four hours for your entire date, go shopping together and then assemble the meals. If you only have a couple hours for your date, buy the ingredients ahead of time and use your date to simply assemble them together.

Assign jobs to each person. For example, one person cuts the veggies while the other person measures the spices.

Additional Idea: If you make multiples of each recipe, you can keep some for yourselves and give some to others, such as a busy family member, a coworker, or your child's teacher. You could also save some for an occasion when someone has a baby or surgery.

Cooking can be drab, but this date is meant to be fun. To lighten the mood for the task, turn on some music and bring your sense of humor to the kitchen!

FOR CONVERSATION:

- What do you miss most about childhood?

- What is the most interesting documentary you have watched?

- What do you think is the weirdest thing about the opposite sex?

- Do you have any daily rituals? Do they help you or do you feel trapped by them?

- What most annoys you?

- Could you still be content if I put more time and energy into developing my talents further if it meant less time and energy for you?

HANDMADE GIFT FOR PARENTS

Together, make a gift for your parents (or a parental figure) to give them at Christmas.

Ideas: a painted canvas, a wreath, an address wall planter, a bird feeder, a door mat with a personalized message, a personalized ceramic pot for plants, a book of encouragement for their bad days. For more ideas, browse the hobby store.

FOR CONVERSATION:

- If someone from the 1800's visited us, what would be the hardest thing for them to get used to?

- What would they be most excited about? What would they be most distraught over?

- If you were given a 25th hour in your day and could use it only to pursue an art, which art form would you choose?

- What is something you learned this week?

- Which three people do you most trust?

- In what ways are we, as husband and wife, most compatible?

OILY DATE

Set aside a couple hours and ensure the kids are either at a sitter's house or tucked *soundly* in bed for this date. You will need:

- a bottle of oil (massage oil or coconut oil)
- an old sheet you won't mind getting oily
- candles (optional)
- music (optional)
- blindfold (optional)

Spread the sheet out on the floor. If you're comfortable using a blindfold, you can use it for some, or all, of the date. Cover your spouse in oil—every inch—paying attention to details and contours. Don't be sparse with the oil! Use it lavishly so your spouse's whole body is super slick! Then choose some, or all, of these activities:

- Dance together with much body contact—fast, slow, or both.

- Experiment with various touches—drumming, stroking, scratching, kneading. Use different parts of your body to massage your spouse—fingers, hands, forearms, feet.

- Play Copycat—Sit cross-legged facing each other. Copy how your spouse touches you by touching him or her that way. Take turns being the copycat. P.S. Highly recommend the blindfold for this as it heightens senses. P.P.S. This is a good way to teach your spouse what you like!

- After you've had fun to max capacity (wink, wink), enjoy cuddling your oily spouse with full-body contact.

- Write loving words on your spouse's back while he or she guesses what you're writing.

- Scrub each other down in the shower at the end of the date. (Caution: the shower floor will be slipperier than usual!)

FOR CONVERSATION:

- If you had the power to spread one of these wherever you went, which would you choose: joy, peace, healing?

- If a stranger walked through your home, what would they conclude about you?

- If someone looked at your checkbook and spending habits, what would they believe you most value?

- What is one thing I have done for you that helped you tremendously?

- If we were to take a class together, what class would you want to take?

- What do you miss most about me when I'm away?

- What is your favorite intimate memory with me?

DECEMBER

CHRISTMAS SHOPPING

Go Christmas shopping together. In addition to checking off a few people from your list of family and friends, add one more person. Use December's budgeted date money to buy a gift for a child or family in an unfortunate circumstance.

> While you're shopping, make sure to point out to your spouse some things you like. Maybe he or she would love a hint.

FOR CONVERSATION:

- If you were given a month away in a cabin for the purpose of resting your soul, what would you do?

- What do you think is the most valuable lesson you can teach others from your past experiences?

- What was the last thing you prayed about?

- What was the most disappointing gift you opened as a child?

- What has been the most thoughtful gift you have received at Christmas?

- What feelings does Christmas bring up inside you—positive or negative?

- Name five things you appreciate about your spouse.

CHRISTMAS PHOTO SHOOT

Prop up your phone and set it to self-timer mode for a Christmas photo shoot of just the two of you.

Ideas:

- Decorating the Christmas tree
- Wrapped in a blanket and cozied-up by an outdoor fire
- Wrapped together in Christmas lights
- Walking by a nativity scene
- Walking through a Christmas tree farm
- Holding or sipping from your favorite Christmas mugs
- Snuggling by the fireplace in Christmas pajamas
- Playing in the snow
- Holding two candy canes together to form a heart
- Decorated in Santa hats
- Being silly in your ugly sweaters
- Dancing by the tree
- Decorating cookies

FOR CONVERSATION:

- What is something you will never try again?

- What one thing about you does your extended family disapprove?

- What are you curious about?

- What is the weirdest thing you have witnessed at work?

- Did you ever have the awkward moment of receiving a gift but hadn't bought one for the giver?

- What tradition would you love to bring into our Christmas?

- Wives: Would you rather wear a sexy dress on a date or a simple, comfortable dress?

- Husbands: Do you most enjoy seeing your wife's front or back?

HIKING IN A WINTER WONDERLAND

Bundle up and go hiking in the wintery woods or on a nearby walking trail. A break with nature is good in the bustling Christmas season. If snow is possible this month, try planning this date for when there would be freshly fallen snow. However, if snow is not a possibility, the winter woods still have a serenity about them, even without snow. While walking through the woods, take in the stillness of nature. Look for animal tracks. If it snowed, aim snowballs at a tree trunk or make little snowmen.

Afterward, have a hot cocoa taste test. Ahead of time, buy a few different kinds of hot cocoa. You could buy a variety pack or search online for creative hot cocoa mix recipes. If you have remaining hot cocoa mix, put them in jars to give away as gifts.

FOR CONVERSATION:

- Do you ever feel alone in a room full of people?

- What is your favorite Christmas song?

- If there were no expectations on Christmas, how would you prefer to spend the day?

- What are the strengths in your marriage? What are its weaknesses? How can we improve the weaknesses?

- Describe what would make the most amazing sex.

TENT TALK & GOAL SETTING

Remember when you made tents in your living room as a child? Build a tent with your spouse by hanging sheets over furniture. Or take the easy route and drape the sheets over your table. To add ambience, string Christmas lights throughout your tent. Fill the tent with blankets and pillows. Crawl inside and discuss goals for the New Year. Questions for self-reflection are included for you to think through individually—to spur thoughts about where you are and where you want to be. Then, together, go through the discussion questions.

QUESTIONS FOR SELF-REFLECTION:

- What legacy do you want to leave? Are you on track for that?

- Do your actions align with the values deep in your heart?

- If there was no possibility of failure, what change would you love to see in yourself this year?

- Does the time you spend outside your job reflect your priorities well?

- Are you where you want to be in your career?

- In what area could you benefit from increasing your knowledge by simply reading a book or taking a class?

- Are you financially where you want to be? Give thought to paying down debts, saving, and investing.

- How could you improve spiritually? Consider: faith, trust, time spent with God, sin in your life, sharing your faith.

- Are there any unhealthy habits lingering in your life?

- In what ways might people in your life benefit from you kicking that habit?

- Sometimes, we can't simply eliminate a habit without replacing it with a healthier habit. Consider a healthy replacement.

- What risks are involved with your dreams?

- Weigh up the risks versus the benefit.

- What relationship needs improvement or your forgiveness?

- Who in your life could use a little more encouragement?

- Are there healthy changes in your eating habits or exercise routine you feel are possible?

- In what ways are your comfort zones limiting you?

- What triumph would most make you proud if you accomplished it by the end of the year?

- What is your life purpose? Are you there? What needs to happen to get you on track for your life purpose?

QUESTIONS FOR DISCUSSION:

- In going through the questions for self-reflection, what unexpected thoughts came to mind?

- Were there any questions that stirred a desire in you that you didn't realize you had?

- Were there questions that made you realize you aren't where you want to be?

- What limits you in achieving where you want to be?

- What sacrifices are you ready to make?

- What goals have you ultimately decided to make into a New Year's resolution?

- How can I help you achieve those goals?

CONCLUSION

We hope you were able to find new ways of connecting and were brought closer together on this dating journey. If you haven't already, consider participating in the full package of Marriage In Abundance, including marriage challenges and couples' devotions. Find out how by visiting www.marriageinabundance.com. Stay tuned as there will be a second book with another year of fun and bonding activities coming soon!

APPENDIX

IDEAS FOR WINNER'S PRIZE:

- Winner chooses the next movie.

- Winner receives a massage from Loser.

- Loser does one of Winner's typical chores next week.

- Loser makes the meal of Winner's choosing.

- Winner gets a morning to sleep-in.

- Winner gets three hours of free time while Loser watches the kids.

- Winner gets a sexual favor from Loser.

FOREPLAY SCAVENGER HUNT

WIFE'S INSTRUCTIONS FOR PLACING CLUES:

Be sure you have candles and a lighter to hide with the clues. Tip for hiding the clues: Don't make them too difficult to find. There will be twelve stops with foreplay building at each stop. Clues hidden too difficult will only frustrate and kill the mood. Since this is not a Winner vs. Loser competition, it is suggested to hide the clues in places somewhat easy to find.

Where to hide your clues:

- Hold on to Clue #1. You will give it to your husband to start the game.

- Put Clue #2 where your clothes get cleaned, whether it's in, or near, the washing machine or, if you use a laundromat, with your bottle of laundry detergent.

- Put Clue #3 with his tools, specifically his hammer.

- Put Clue #4 in the checkbook that's used to pay the bills.

- Put Clue #5 in the car your husband drives.

- Put Clue #6 in the bathroom guests use. Also, hide the candles and lighter with this clue.

- Put Clue #7 inside your favorite book (your, the wife's, favorite book).

FOREPLAY SCAVENGER HUNT

HUSBAND'S INSTRUCTIONS FOR PLACING CLUES:

Be sure you have the massage oil (or coconut oil), and the "food for licking" to hide with the clues. Tip for hiding the clues: Don't make them too difficult to find. There will be twelve stops with foreplay building at each stop. Clues hidden too difficult will only frustrate and kill the mood. Since this is not a Winner vs. Loser competition, it is suggested to hide the clues in places somewhat easy to find.

Where to hide your clues:

- Put Clue #8 with your typical breakfast of choice (your, the husband's, breakfast choice).

- Put Clue #9 in her bra or underwear drawer.

- Put Clue #10 where you plug in your phone at night (you, the husband).

- Put Clue #11 in the shower your wife uses. Also, hide the food-for-licking in the shower with the clue.

- Put Clue #12 under her side of the bed. Also, hide the massage or coconut oil under the bed with the clue. (Careful! Dogs love coconut oil.)

- #13 Tape or pin this "last stop" clue on one of her fancy dresses, being careful not to ruin the dress.

CLUES FOR FOREPLAY SCAVENGER HUNT

Tear out the next page and cut up the clues (without reading them if you like surprises). Give the clues labeled 1-7 to the wife to hide and the clues labeled 8-12 to the husband to hide.

If you are reading an e-book or have borrowed this book from the library, follow the instructions in Appendix E to make your own clues.

CLUE #1

Your first stop, I *propose*
is where we clean our *clothes*.

CLUE #2

I hope this is clear and I don't
stammer. Where do you go to find
your *h-h-hammer?*

CLUE #3

For your next clue and more cheap
thrills, look in that thing we use to
pay *bills*.

CLUE #4

To venture beyond home...if you *dare*,
this is your method to get *there*.

CLUE #5

If a guest comes over and needs
privacy, they will go to this room,
you *see*.

CLUE #6

For more romance, go take a *look*.
It may be in your wife's favorite *book*.

CLUE #7

(Wife solves this and the remainder.)
In the morning, if he's in a *mood*,
show him where to find his typical
breakfast *food*.

CLUE #8

This clothing of yours...
      it's private for most.
   He's seen it before.
   It's in that drawer.

CLUE #9

Yes, it's getting hot! Don't get
uptight! Next clue's in the spot, he
charges his phone at *night*.

CLUE #10

Close to the potty. But that's not
exactly it. It's where you clean your
body, when you've got *grit*.

CLUE #11

Don't give up, let's take another
leap. The next clue is under the
place you count *sheep!*

CLUE #12

If you went to a pricy restaurant
and *dancing*, you might wear this
special dress that is *fancy*.

CLUE #13

Last stop

Discuss your favorite positions or fantasies, and your comfort level regarding each other's fantasies. Agree on what you will do when you reach the end of the scavenger hunt.	
Kiss for 60 seconds while sliding your hands underneath each other's clothes for a little teasing.	Kiss her neck, passionately, for 30-60 seconds.
Take the candles to the place you want to end your date.	Make out in the backseat of the car for 5-10 minutes, leaving clothes on. It's not yet time to go all the way! But you may pet and grind.
Turn on the slow dancing music and dance. Kiss through every chorus.	What is your favorite song for slow dancing? Get it queued up and ready.
Move sexy for him by swinging your hips in sultry figure eights, gliding your hands up and down your torso (and every place on your body you know *he* would love to have *his* hands). You can strip off any remaining clothing in the process.	Take off your clothes (or have your spouse do it for you), keeping on any sexy undergarments.
While hugging in a tight embrace, massage the oil all over each other's backs. Then release your embrace and cover the fronts of each other.	Remove any remaining clothes. Then, smear the "food for licking" on each other and enjoy!
	This is the end of the scavenger hunt, but not the end of your night! Time to gratify.

INSTRUCTIONS FOR WRITING OUT YOUR OWN FOREPLAY SCAVENGER HUNT CLUES

Cut out 13 pieces of paper. Give seven to the wife and six to the husband. Each follow the respective instructions.

WIFE'S INSTRUCTIONS FOR WRITING OUT CLUES

On each piece of paper, write:

- On the front, write, "Clue #1: Your first stop, I propose is where we clean our clothes." Leave the back blank. Give this to your husband at the beginning of the hunt.

- On the front, write, "Clue #2: I hope this is clear and I don't stammer. Where do you go to find your h-h-hammer?" On the back, write, "Discuss your favorite positions or fantasies, and your comfort level regarding each other's fantasies. Agree on what you will do when you reach the end of the scavenger hunt."

- On the front, write, "Clue #3: For your next clue and more cheap thrills, look in that thing we use to pay bills." On the back, write, "Kiss her neck, passionately, for thirty to sixty seconds."

- On the front, write, "Clue #4: To venture beyond home…

if you dare, this is your method to get there." On the back, write, "Kiss for sixty seconds while sliding your hands underneath each other's clothes for a little teasing."

- On the front, write, "Clue #5: If a guest comes over and needs privacy, they will go to this room, you see." On the back, write, "Make out in the backseat of the car for five to ten minutes, leaving clothes on. It's not yet time to go all the way! But you may pet and grind."

- On the front, write, "Clue #6: For more romance, go take a look. It may be in your wife's favorite book." On the back, write, "Take the candles to the place you want to end your date."

- On the front, write, "Clue #7: (Wife solves this and the remainder.) In the morning, if he's in a mood, show him where to find his favorite breakfast food." On the back, write, "What is your favorite song for slow dancing? Get it queued up and ready."

HUSBAND'S INSTRUCTIONS FOR WRITING OUT CLUES

On Each piece of paper, write:

- On the front, write, "Clue #8: This clothing of yours… it's private for most. He's seen it before. It's in that drawer." On the back, write, "Turn on the slow dancing music and dance. Kiss through every chorus."

- On the front, write, "Clue #9: Yes, it's getting hot! Don't get uptight! Next clue's in the spot, he charges his phone at night." On the back, write, "Take off your clothes (or have your spouse do it for you), keeping on any sexy undergarments."

- On the front, write, "Clue #10: Close to the potty. But that's not *exactly* it. It's where you clean your body, when you've got grit." On the back, write, "Move sexy for him by swinging your hips in sultry figure eights, gliding your hands up and down your torso (and every place on your body you know *he* would love to have *his* hands). You can strip off any remaining clothing in the process."

- On the front, write, "Clue #11: Don't give up, let's take another leap. The next clue is under the place you count sheep!" On the back, write, "Remove any remaining clothes. Then, smear the 'food for licking' on each other and enjoy!"

- On the front, write, "Clue #12: If you went to a pricy restaurant and dancing, you might wear this special dress that is fancy." On the back, write, "While hugging in a tight embrace, massage the oil all over each other's backs. Then release your embrace and cover the fronts of each other."

- On the front, write, "Clue #13: Last Stop." On the back, write, "This is the end of the scavenger hunt, but not the end of your night! Time to gratify."

WINTER CONSTELLATIONS OF THE NORTHERN HEMISPHERE

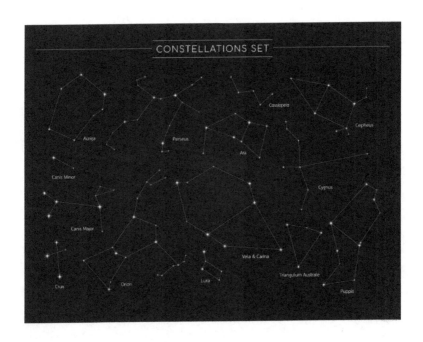

BOUDOIR PHOTO SHOOT

A BOUDOIR PHOTO SHOOT OF HER, TAKEN BY HIM.

A note to the ladies:

Before chucking this date in the trash, read on to discover how it can be modified to meet the comfort level of anyone and everyone, no matter your body type or age.

First off, don't let the world tell you what is beautiful! God only creates beauty.

You are beautiful!

If you have a full figure, you are curvaceous and wonderful. If you have scars or stretch marks, you have a reminder of what made you into the strong woman you are. If your body has been around for seventy years, you have lines formed by many smiles and tears. You have a body to be appreciated for carrying you through all the experiences that brought you where you are today. If you have a feature that's different from others, be proud of your diversity!

The world has pushed us all to believe there is *only one* standard of beauty for *all of us* to meet. Let's not accept that but push past the agenda that stems from a twisted industry. Believing this lie preserves a narrow and twisted ideology. Let's blow it to bits!

Women are their own worst critics. But a man tends to see beauty in his wife where she cannot. Believe us, we've talked to many men who simply want their woman to see the same beauty he sees in her.

Men are visual. A man *wants* to see his wife's body. And God designed marriage for us to enjoy one another's bodies! This photo shoot is a gift for him.

What do men find attractive in a woman? Although, they are drawn to inner characteristics like loyalty, a nurturing nature, friendliness, respect, optimism, and compassion, this is a photo shoot and photos don't always capture those qualities. Regarding physical beauty, since each man's preferences are different, find out what your man finds attractive. Then you can give him the most attractive-to-him "you" you can attain. Before you prep for your photo shoot, have your husband fill out the included questionnaire (Appendix H) to learn what "you" he most finds attractive. Then plan your wardrobe, hair, and make-up based on his answers. Select your wardrobe to accentuate his favorite body part(s).

Options for Storing Photos: Before you plan your attire and poses, discuss the comfort level of both you and your husband regarding your photo being taken in private and how you plan to store the photos. There are apps for hidden folders that require a password to access. Another option is to use a polaroid camera and keep the photos locked in a safe. If your husband is artistic, you could show him a few poses, ask him to choose his favorite, and then pose that way while he sketches you. If you feel saving suggestive photos in any way is too risky, dress in a way that would not embarrass you if your photos were to be found by your kids or a stranger, but also in a way that would lift his spirits on a bad day!

For a photo shoot only for him, there needs to be a deep level of trust. He needs to agree ahead of time to give you the freedom to access the photos and to delete the ones you don't like or go beyond your comfort zone.

Wardrobe options: There are many options. Nudity is not a requirement to snap a photo he will cherish!

If the thought of your naked (or almost naked) body in a photo stresses you out, here are some other great options: an oversized shirt or sweater falling off your shoulder, short shorts and a lacy top, low-cut jeans and a crop top hanging off the shoulder, a fitted tank top and a high-slit skirt, a tight dress, *his* shirt buttoned only once, tight jeans and a low-cut top. The poses described here will be *sizzlin'* in even the most modest clothes!

If the idea of your revealing photos does not stress you out and **there is a deep level of trust between you and your hubby, try:** sexy lingerie, a corset, a sexy bra and panties (with the strap falling off the shoulder in some shots), a silky robe loosely tied, a see-through shirt, a wet, white t-shirt, completely nude, or nothing but a string of pearls and high heels. Alternatively, you could shoot in the nude but keep your privates covered by crossing your legs, or by using your long hair if you have it, or by keeping an arm or hand over just those areas. Another option is to remain nude but keep a crumpled-up sheet or fuzzy blanket nearby and drape it over the places you want to cover in each photo.

But I'm insecure about….my poochy tummy, my flat chest, my lumpy, cellulite legs…fill in the blank. If it makes you feel more confident to cover up areas of insecurity, then do so. However, remember most men don't see flaws the way women see flaws in themselves. Go through the poses in front of a mirror to see which ones work best for your body type—bending and stretching in certain ways can paint certain areas in a different light.

We have included instructions for a wide array of poses from slightly suggestive to risqué and erotic. Practice the poses alone, ahead of time, in front of a mirror. Go through every single pose. If you don't like the way your body looks in one of the first poses, don't chuck every step thereafter. You may find one of the later poses portrays your best features well.

Mark the poses you feel good about and want to show your husband later. Practice each pose with different "outfits" to see which attire works best for each pose and which combination accentuates the features your husband most loves.

Optional Props: Blanket, fur rug, jewelry, a sign with your husband's name or a message for him, your wedding veil or garter, flowers, his tie, a football jersey, his hobby such as a guitar or football, a stool, a large mirror.

Other Fun Tips:

- Posing in front of a mirror can give a view of both your front and your back in the same shot.

- A tub full of bubbles makes for a fun scene! Go for nude with bubbles covering your privates or the wet t-shirt look.

- If you are artistic, you can use body paint to decorate your body.

- Use lighting to your advantage. Dim the lights and use a soft glowing light or candle to light up your curves or pose in the dark with a light behind you, which turns your body into a silhouette.

- For hand placement, here are sexy places he likes to see your hands: in your hair, on your chest between your neck and breasts, on your breasts, at your panty line, slightly under your clothes as if you're about to take them off, or on your neck when your head is looking down.

- Try gazing in various directions. Looking directly at the camera gives a look of confidence. Looking down gives a look of approachability. A dreamy, soft gaze can be attained by looking far off in the distance.

- Keep your face—lips, jaw, and brows—relaxed. Otherwise, you look stressed.

- Have your husband focus some shots on your full body and some shots zoomed in on just your face. He may want to vary the angle of the camera in each pose.

- Focusing on the face with the body blurred in the background gives a look of intrigue.

Set Your Mood: It helps to get in a sensual mood ahead of time. Set the tone with sultry music. Sway your hips in a "figure-eight." Softly brush your hands along your sides or wherever else feels sexy. If you don't prepare your mood, you may end up laughing your way through, which isn't the worst thing! Decide what kind of mood you want to bring into your photos and prepare yourself for that. To keep it sexy and smooth, instruct your hubby to cover his eyes or turn around in between the poses.

Disclaimer: Don't bend your body in ways it is not used to. Many of the poses are made sexy through arching your back. If you tend to have back issues, skip that part. Don't pull a muscle over this!

One More Message to Women: One of the most important aspects to be portrayed to your husband is confidence. Men are attracted to confidence! Take on the mindset that you are beautiful, and you have *Got. It. Going. On.* With this attitude, your husband will agree you have something to be proud of. It's easy to spot a yellow car when we're looking for a yellow car. It's easy to spot a flaw when a woman points it out. But, when a woman displays confidence about her qualities, that is what her husband will see. Make your husband believe, as he truly should, he has the cream of the crop!

It's time to take your sexy back.

POSES

Poses Using a Stool

1. Sit on a stool. Place both hands around one knee and slightly pick up that knee, keeping the other knee straight. Have him take a shot from the front and from the side.

2. Place your hands on the sides of the stool and slide your bum to the very edge (like you might fall off if your hands weren't supporting you). Keep your arms straight and legs straight, except for one knee slightly bent. Pop your chest out and tip your head back so it's facing the ceiling. Have him take a shot from the side or diagonally front/side. Then have him zoom in on just your face and upper torso.

3. Now sit normal on the stool. Look down and place your hand (with your wedding ring) between your neck and chest. Have him zoom in on just your hand, neck, and chest.

Poses Using a Sheet (Nude Underneath)

4. Sit on a stool facing away from him. Drape the sheet around the back of you and let it fall/droop to show off your back. Look behind you and give an innocent smile.

5. Set the stool aside. Stand with your back to him. While holding the sheet, stretch your arms up and out to your sides, allowing it to droop enough to show some of your back. (This makes an intriguing silhouette when you place a light in front of you and he takes a shot from behind you.)

6. Face your husband or have him diagonally at your side. Wrap the sheet around you and let it fall wherever you want to give him a peek.

7. Wrap the sheet tight around your chest to give you cleavage. Allow a leg to peek out of a slit.

Poses Standing

8. Standing, cross your arms across your breasts, shrug your right shoulder up while looking down and to the right.

9. Stand with him at a diagonal to you. Bend, slightly, at your waist and place your hands on your thighs, keeping your arms straight. Arch your back so you butt is popped out. If you're wearing a bra, shrugging your shoulders up will reveal more cleavage.

10. Stand upright. Shift most of your weight onto one leg. Place one hand between your legs and the other hand behind your head.

11. Tap your left leg out to the side, popping your right hip up as far as it will go. Place your right hand on your right hip and left hand in your hair. Look down and to the right.

12. Stand with your back to your hubby. Pop your butt and chest out. Turn slightly so he can get a slight view of the front. Grab the top of your waist band or place your hand where it *would* be.

Poses Using a Wall

13. Stand with your back leaning against a wall, your feet about a foot from the wall, and your husband to your left side. Bend slightly at your hips and knees. Keeping your shoulders and bum against the wall, give your low back a slight arch. Put your arms above your head and get a shot. Then place your left hand on your left hip and your right hand on your neck and get a shot.

14. Keep your bum and head against the wall but arch your back to bring your back and shoulders aways from the wall. Place your hands over your breasts. Tip your head up to look toward the ceiling.

15. Turn to face the wall. Position your feet a couple feet away from the wall. Lean into the wall, supporting yourself with your forearms against it (hands above your head). Slightly bend one knee, keeping your other leg straight. Arch your back to pop your bum out and breasts out. Have him take a shot from the side and from behind.

16. Still facing the wall, but no longer leaning on your forearms, place only your hands/palms on the wall above your head. Point your bum out toward him (behind you), and slightly bend one knee. Look back over your shoulder at him.

17. Stay in this position but step your feet apart a couple feet.

Poses Sitting on the Floor

18. Sit on the floor with your back to your hubby. Bend your knees to your chest. Hug your arm around your knees and look off to the side. Have your hubby take a shot of your full body from behind and a close-up of just your face looking over your shoulder.

19. Have your hubby come around to your side. Stay seated with your knees bent about 90 degrees, feet still on the floor. Bend your upper body so your chest is touching your thighs. Stretch your arms to reach toward your feet. Give your hubby an "I want you" look.

20. Have your hubs come around to your front. Wrap one arm around your knees and pull them just slightly up toward your chest. Cross your legs at your ankles and use your legs and feet to cover your privates. One arm is around your legs and the other arm is reaching to its opposite shoulder/ upper arm. Look to the side and down.

21. Lay your left leg (with knee bent) down in front of you, like cross-legged position but only one leg. Slide your right foot to the right, keeping your right knee bent. Lay your right

leg, with knee bent, out to your right side so your foot is near your bum behind you. Turn your upper body to the left slightly, pop your chest out and place your left hand near your bottom and your right hand on your right knee.

22. Keep your legs in this position. Lean to the left and support yourself with your straight left arm, popping your left shoulder up a bit. Place your right hand on your right knee with your arm straight. Look to the right and reach your chin toward your right shoulder, looking down at your right leg. Your right hand can be on your right leg, behind you, or between your legs in front for a sultry pose.

23. Stay here with your legs in this position but shift your weight forward and up off the floor, over your left foot. Your crotch should be about six inches from the floor. (Note: you are not really sitting anymore.) Place your right hand on your right thigh and your left hand in your hair. Look to the left.

24. With your husband at your right side, sit on your feet with your knees bent and together. (Your shins are on the floor.) Touch the back of your head with both hands, elbows pointing up. Turn slightly to face him. Arch your back and pop your chest out.

25. Stay seated like this on your feet with your shins on the ground and husband at your side. Place your hands on your knees, lean forward, popping your chest out. Tip your head up.

26. While still seated on your feet, lean back, supporting your body with your hands behind you. Arch your back and pop your chest out. Tip your head up.

27. Still in this position, keep your right hand on the ground behind you but place your left hand behind your head and turn slightly to the right.

28. With your knees still out in front of you, come up on

your toes into a squat so your bum is sitting on your heels. Spread your knees apart. Drop your straight arms between your legs to the floor. Have your hubs take a shot directly in front and then diagonally from behind while you twist toward him.

Poses Lying on the Floor

29. Lie on your right side with your back to your hubby. Support your upper body with your right forearm, knees slightly bent, and look back at him over your left shoulder. Give him a sultry look.

30. Now lie on your stomach with your hubby still at your right side, or diagonally in front of you. Prop yourself up on your elbows and bend your knees. Give him a look that sizzles.

31. Keep your upper body propped on your elbows. Slightly bend your right knee and lay it somewhat out to the side. Give him a steamy look.

32. If you're flexible enough, while still on your stomach with your hubby to your right, bring your legs back together and straighten them. Push your upper body up with your hands, keeping your elbows straight. (Left arm can slightly bend at the elbow.) Give him a look that says you love his touches.

33. Lie on your back. Stretch your straight arms out at your sides on the ground, like a snow angel. Bend one leg at the knee. Arch your back and pop your chest out. Tell him with your eyes that you want him. Have your hubs take a shot from the side and then have him move toward your head (feet further from him) and take a shot from that angle.

34. Remain lying there on your back but bend your elbows and place your hands under your head. Lift your legs straight up, pointing your toes to the ceiling, slightly bending one leg. Have him take shots from where he is at the head and also from the side.

35. While on your back, bend both your knees and lay them together to your left side. Place your hands in your hair at the top of your head. Twist your upper body to the right. He can take a shot from the head, left side, and right side.

36. Place both your feet on the floor, hands behind your head, and arch your back and bum up, like bridge position. Try moving to your tiptoes in this position.

Poses in Other Positions on the Floor

37. Get on all fours, but instead of your hands and knees, get on your elbows and knees. Slightly crawl one leg forward and the other slightly back. Have him take shots from in front of you and diagonally.

38. Remain in this position. Keeping both elbows on the ground, turn your head to the right and place your left hand in your hair. He can get a full-body and a close-up of just your head.

39. Stay on your knees but bring them closer together. Turn so he is at your head, your feet are further from him. Drop your chest to the ground while keeping your bum in the air. Bend your elbows, laying your forearms on the floor, and rest your head on your hands. Have him lower the camera near the floor in front of you.

Poses Sitting on the Bed

40. Sit on the edge of the bed. Keeping your feet on the floor, straighten your knees. Use your straight arms behind you to prop yourself up as you scoot your bum very close to the edge of the bed. You can slightly bend and twist one knee or cross your ankles. He can get a shot from the front, from the side, and from behind.

41. Now sit on the edge of the bed normally, so you're not falling off. Place your arms at your sides, elbows straight,

hands touching the bed. Bring your knees together but your feet apart. Look to the side and down.

Poses Lying on the Bed

42. Lie across the bed sideways—partially on your stomach, partially on your side—upper knee slightly bent. Have your husband squat near your head and take a shot from that angle and then from the side.

43. Lie flat on your stomach. Turn your head to the side to look at him. Stretch your arms overhead, then bend one elbow (the one closest to him), putting that hand in your hair.

44. Lie on your back on the bed with your bum scooted up near the headboard. Lift your feet up toward the ceiling and lay your legs against the headboard. Cross your ankles.

45. Staying on your back, scoot toward the foot of the bed until your head is dangling off the edge. Have your husband squat near your head. Bend one knee. You can cross your arms under your breasts, like a hug for yourself, or you can lay your arms out to your sides like a snow angel.

Poses Using the Bed as a Prop

46. Stand with your back to the bed and your feet about 2 feet from the bed. Squat down so your bum is about 6 inches from the floor. Lay your upper body and head back on the bed. Bring your arms up over your head and lay them down on the bed as if you're slowly sliding off the bed. Lift your heels up so your weight is on your toes. Look at him lustfully.

47. Stay squatting and leaning your shoulders against the bed but place your straight arms on your thighs and tip your head back.

HUSBAND'S PREPARATORY QUESTIONNAIRE FOR BOUDOIR PHOTO SHOOT

- What is your favorite lingerie of mine?

- What is your favorite body part of mine?

- Which hairstyle of mine do you find sexiest? Up in a ponytail? Down? Curly? Straight?

- Do you prefer dark, heavy make-up, light make-up, or all natural?

- What object or shirt of yours would you find sexy for me to wear or hold? (For ex: jersey, guitar, football, a specific shirt…)

SECOND-HAND STORE SCAVENGER HUNT LISTS

FOR THE HUSBAND

- Book with a cat on the cover (2 points)
- Toy you owned when you were a kid (3 points)
- Striped throw pillow (1 point)
- Bunny stuffed animal (1 point)
- Welcome sign (1 point)
- Coffee mug with Scripture (2 points)
- Necktie with a sports theme (2 points)
- Leopard print blazer (3 points)
- Flowery swim trunks (1 point)
- Dog costume (2 points)
- Shirt with a picture of a dinosaur (2 points)
- Red purse (1 point) If it is red *and* snakeskin pattern (3 points)
- Football jersey (1 point)
- Shirt with the name of the city or town you live in (2 points)
- Red, white, and blue baseball pants (1 point)

- Baby blanket with African animals, such as a monkey, elephant, giraffe, or zebra (1 point for a blanket with one African animal, 2 points for two or three African animals, 3 points for four or more African animals)

- Shirt with a school name: college (1 point), elementary (2 points), jr. high or high school (3 points)

- Pants or shorts with these three colors: red, yellow, and blue (2 points) If they *only* have those three colors and no other colors (3 points)

- Santa or a picture of Santa (1 point)

- Easter décor (1 point)

- Movie based on a Bible story (2 points)

- Basket any color other than brown, tan, or gray (1 point)

- Yard game (1 point)

- Pool toy (1 point)

- Sparkly high heels (1 point) If they are sparkly *and* purple (3 points)

- Shirt with a picture of a wolf (2 points)

- Puzzle with a dog on it (2 points)

- Barbie, or other doll, with hair that's *not* a natural color such as brown, black, blonde, auburn, or strawberry blonde (2 points)

- Marriage book (2 points)

- Cookbook of only desserts (2 points)

FOR THE WIFE

- Book with a cat on the cover (2 points)
- Toy you owned when you were a kid (3 points)
- Striped throw pillow (1 point)
- Bunny stuffed animal (1 point)
- Welcome sign (1 point)
- Coffee mug with Scripture (2 points)
- Necktie with a sports theme (2 points)
- Leopard print blazer (3 points)
- Flowery swim trunks (1 point)
- Dog costume (2 points)
- Shirt with a picture of a dinosaur (2 points)
- Red purse (1 point) If it is red *and* snakeskin pattern (3 points)
- Football jersey (1 point)
- Shirt with the name of the city or town you live in (2 points)
- Red, white, and blue baseball pants (1 point)
- Baby blanket with African animals, such as a monkey, elephant, giraffe, or zebra (1 point for a blanket with one African animal, 2 points for two or three African animals, 3 points for four or more African animals)
- Shirt with a school name: college (1 point), elementary (2 points), jr. high or high school (3 points)
- Pants or shorts with these three colors: red, yellow, and blue (2 points) If they *only* have those three colors and no other colors (3 points)
- Santa or a picture of Santa (1 point)

- Easter décor (1 point)
- Movie based on a Bible story (2 points)
- Basket any color other than brown, tan, or gray (1 point)
- Yard game (1 point)
- Pool toy (1 point)
- Sparkly high heels (1 point) If they are sparkly *and* purple (3 points)
- Shirt with a picture of a wolf (2 points)
- Puzzle with a dog on it (2 points)
- Barbie, or other doll, with hair that's *not* a natural color such as brown, black, blonde, auburn, or strawberry blonde (2 points)
- Marriage book (2 points)
- Cookbook of only desserts (2 points)

RECIPES FOR FREEZER MEALS

First, label your gallon freezer bags using permanent marker—the date it was prepared, the name of the recipe, and the instructions for heating the day it will be cooked.

ITALIAN LEMON CHICKEN

Write directions on the freezer bag: "Cook in crock pot on low for 4-6 hours or in the oven at 375° for 30 minutes. If cooking in the oven, thaw ahead of time."

Ingredients:
- 2 pounds boneless chicken breasts
- ¼ cup lemon juice
- 1/3 cup olive oil
- ½ tsp of each: basil, garlic powder, oregano, onion powder, black pepper, paprika, salt

BEEF & CABBAGE SOUP

Write directions on the freezer bag: "Add 4 cups of beef broth to the crock pot on day of cooking. Cook on low for 8 hours."

Ingredients:

　　1 pound ground beef*
　　1 small cabbage, cut up
　　1 onion, diced
　　4 cloves garlic, minced
　　2 cups, or handfuls, baby carrots
　　14.5 oz can diced tomatoes, undrained
　　2 tsp salt
　　1 tsp pepper
　　4 c beef broth (Do not add to freezer bag. Simply make sure
　　　　you have it on day of cooking.)

　　*Ground beef can be added to the freezer bag raw but will cook in chunks. For better consistency, brown it prior to adding it to the freezer bag.

BEEF & VEGETABLE SOUP

Write directions on the freezer bag: "Add 4 cups of beef broth to the crock pot on day of cooking. Cook on low 8 hours."

Ingredients:

1 pound ground beef*
24 oz jar spaghetti sauce
1 onion, diced
2 cups, or handfuls, baby carrots, sliced
2 cups green beans
2 cups corn
1 zucchini, sliced
1 T salt
4 cups beef broth (Do not add to freezer bag. Simply make sure you have it on day of cooking.)

*Ground beef can be added to freezer bag raw but will cook in chunks. For better consistency, brown it prior to adding it to the freezer bag.

CHICKEN VEGETABLE SOUP

Write directions on the freezer bag: "Add 2 cups chicken broth to the crock pot on day of cooking. Cook on low for 8 hours. At the end of cooking, remove the chicken, cut it into bite-size chunks, and put it back in."

Ingredients:

1 pound boneless chicken breasts
2 cups frozen vegetables, any vegetable you like
2 sweet potatoes, cut into 1-inch cubes
1 onion, diced
2 - 15 oz can diced tomatoes, undrained
3 T tomato paste
4 T balsamic vinegar
4 cloves garlic, minced
2 tsp oregano
½ tsp rosemary
¼ tsp thyme
¼ tsp red pepper flakes
¼ tsp ground pepper
2 tsp salt
2 cups chicken broth (Do not add to freezer bag. Simply make sure you have it on day of cooking.)

ABOUT THE AUTHOR

Mandy Shrock is the founder of Marriage In Abundance, a ministry aimed at deepening the bonds of married couples. In addition to writing materials for marriage improvement, she also wrote, *Life In Abundance,* devotions for anyone, no matter their stage in life. She is passionate about life, the Word of God, marriage, sci-fi and fantasy books, exercise, the outdoors, natural foods, and dogs. Powered by coffee, she lives with her husband, four children, and two dogs in northern Indiana.

Made in United States
Troutdale, OR
04/25/2024

19446922R00106